VINTAGE MOTORCARS

David Burgess Wise

VINTAGE MOTORCARS

Illustrations by Peter Griffin

GROSSET & DUNLAP
A National General Company
Publishers · New York

First published in the United States in 1972 by Grosset & Dunlap, Inc.
© The National Magazine Co. Ltd 1970
Library of Congress Catalog Card Number: 72-159720
ISBN: 0-448-02449-7

Manufactured in Great Britain
ISBN: 0-448-02449-7

Contents

Introduction

'*Motoring Illustrated* suggests the formation of a Motor Museum. If we could be sure that most of the motor omnibuses at present in our streets would find their way there we would gladly subscribe.' Thus wrote that cynical observer, Mr Punch, shortly after the turn of the century. Even then, when motoring had hardly been accepted, when the future of the motorcar was still dubious, the pioneers were attempting to preserve early motorcars for the benefit of posterity. They must have had some inkling of the immense industry that their stuttering horseless carriages would engender, and that future generations might ask 'Where did it all start?'

As early as 1903 an 1895 racing Panhard-Levassor was shown on the stand of the Hon. C. S. Rolls at the Crystal Palace as 'A relic of the past', so rapidly did motorcar design progress in those days: yet now we are accustomed to cars remaining in production in almost unchanged form for ten, even twenty years.

In 1907 the first major historical exhibition of motorcars was organised in conjunction with the Paris Motor Show: forty-five vehicles, built mostly between 1890 and 1900, were displayed, lorded over by the clumsy 1770 Cugnot *fardier*, oldest surviving self-propelled vehicle in the world.

In 1912 *The Motor* set up a motor museum in London: but this was broken up in the Great War, and several of the exhibits destroyed.

Thereafter there were spasmodic attempts to establish motor museums, but none of these really bore fruit until after the Second World War: the preservation of early motorcars was in the hands of private collectors and enlightened motor manufacturing companies.

A newspaper stunt of 1927 resulted in a bunch of aged cars crewed by people in funny hats and false beards motoring from London to Brighton: from this unlikely beginning sprang, three years later, the Veteran Car Club, which found and preserved many old cars. Then, in 1935, came the Vintage Sports Car Club, dedicated to the continued use of the great sporting cars of the 1920s. It was another of those fundamental periods of change, you see, and the cars of the 1930s—although it is becoming heresy to say so now-adays—were not nearly so satisfying to drive, own or maintain as their counterparts of the 1920s.

The cars illustrated in this book cover the whole spectrum of motoring history, from the earliest horseless carriages to the last of the classic sports cars: engine capacities range between under 1000cc and 21.5-litres. Engines crop up in every conceivable position, and there's absolutely no concurrence of opinion as to what form a motorcar should take.

In these conformist days, when two cars can be conceived independently by two designers hundreds of miles apart, and still look as though they have been turned out of the same mould, it is refreshing to see the widely divergent shapes of the pioneer motor-

Introduction

cars. And they are all *honest* shapes: there is none of that conscious striving for effect, that meretricious use of curves and chrome that is the hallmark of the car designed by a committee – not conceived by a single mind – that seeks to turn the curves of a clay mockup into tortured metal. Form has function in the world of the vintage motorcar.

This sincerity of purpose is one reason, I suppose, why we preserve old motorcars: then there is the sense of communion with a healthier past, of recapturing the joys and woes of the pioneers, of learning skills that have grown redundant in a synchromesh age.

Of course these vehicles are becoming more and more costly these days, with little regard to their merits or demerits as cars for driving, but that is really immaterial. The capital gainers who got in on the act because profits on motorcars are not subject to tax will, I suspect, fade away. A car isn't the safest way to lock up your money; it deteriorates so quickly if it isn't cared for properly. Many of the people who own old cars would still cherish them if they were valued, as was the case only a few years ago, in tens rather than thousands of pounds.

Peter Griffin has captured the changing shape of the motorcar by visiting leading public and private collections up and down the country: look at these drawings, and reflect on what we have lost by the over-popularisation of the motorcar. There is still no better mode of transport than a well-set-up vintage touring car: and in terms of door-to-door averages there is often little advantage for the modern car. The vintage machine proceeds about its business with an inexorable steadiness: you have time to enjoy motoring as it should be, and your view of the world is correspondingly clearer.

D B W

1898 Star-Benz

The Star Cycle Company of Wolverhampton was founded in 1883 by Edward Lisle, to build the then fashionable high-wheeled 'ordinary' bicycles. When it turned, in 1898, to the manufacture of motor cars, forming the Star Motor Company, it was natural that the Company should base its designs closely on a well-tried Continental car: at that date the British motor industry was entirely dependent on French and German designs, and the most popular pattern for the copyists was the German Benz. Star took the layout of the Benz pretty much as it had been conceived by Karl Benz, but improved the somewhat minimal cooling system by the addition of a water pump.

The $3\frac{1}{2}$hp engine, with a completely exposed crankshaft, was placed at the rear with its single cylinder pointed forwards. It was started by pulling a massively-spoked flywheel over compression: initial transmission was by flat leather belts running on two pulleys mounted on the crankshaft, which played fast-and-loose to give the choice of ratios; the belts drove a countershaft beneath the driving seat, from which chains drove back to sprockets on the spidery rear wheels.

One of these 'Star-Benz' cars was the first car to be exported to Auckland, New Zealand, in 1898, and was produced in the original Star works in Frederick Street: by 1900 the Star Motor Company had expanded into a warren of cramped back street factories in Dudley Road, Nelson Street, Ablow Street, Frederick Street, Stewart Street and Dobb Street, and were turning out twenty cars each week, and a new twin-cylinder model was produced.

The following years saw the appearance of front-engined models on De Dion and Panhard lines, and then a new cheaper line was introduced under the name of Starling, built under the aegis of the Star Cycle Co. Another new marque name appearing at that time was the Stuart, a rather more substantial brother for the Starlings: but it only lasted two years.

In 1909 the Star Cycle Company changed its name to the Briton Motor Company, becoming more independant of the Star Motor Company, and moved into a newly-built factory between Walsall Street and Willenhall Road. Two models were produced, a 10hp twin and a 14hp four, both high-quality, low-cost cars with excellent performance. In 1910 a 14hp won the silver cup in the Raglan Cup Race at Brooklands at a speed of 65.5 mph.

During the first three decades of this century, Wolverhampton had a considerable motor industry, but most of its great names, including Star, Clyno, Sunbeam, and AJS, vanished in the slump. Briton built a thousand 10hp cars after being reformed in 1922, but then went over to building spares for caterpillar tractors.

1901 Godiva 9hp dos-à-dos

In the early years of the motor age, many small companies – cycle makers, agricultural engineers, gas engine builders – tried their hand at making horseless carriages, then decided there was no future in it, and abandoned the project. One such company was Paynes and Bates Limited, of Foleshill, Coventry, manufacturers of gas engines. In 1900 they built their first car, which they sold under the name of Godiva.

Their main commercial success, however, was the production of a series of cars for R. M. Wright & Co., of Mint Street, Lincoln, who billed themselves as 'Motor and Cycle Makers', and sold the Paynes & Bates cars as 'Stonebows', the name being derived from an ancient gateway in Lincoln.

Basically, these cars followed the well-proven Benz pattern, but were built rather stronger. Even by 1900 the claim that 'the smartest Motor Car on the Market is the Stonebow Motor Dog Cart' was wearing rather thin, but R. M. Wright's sales techniques were quite advanced.

'Don't buy in the dark!' warned their advertising. 'Motor Buyers are *cautioned* against purchasing cars without trying them, simply because they are of a noted make. Cars vary, even in the best makes. We offer customers a FREE TRIAL, a practical test of One Hundred Miles on all sorts of roads.'

The most popular Stonebow model was a single-cylinder four-seater dog-cart with spindly wire wheels, which the agents described in the following ungrammatical terms: 'This car is very modern, very simple, and constructed of the best material and workmanship throughout. The frame is of strong channel steel, fitted with a single cylinder petrol motor 5hp; it is electrically fired, the batteries being carried under the driver's seat, the motor transmits its power to the counter shaft by three belts working on tight and loose pulleys giving three forward speeds and one reverse; the lower speed and reverse are working on to a crypto gear box; the steering is affected by two racks and pinion with a hand wheel on the top of steering post. Coventry chains are used and Clincher Motor Tyres are fitted of the latest pattern; very strong, the whole Car being English made throughout.'

A 7hp version of this car was also made by Paynes and Bates for Wright; but the sole surviving Godiva, a 1901 model, represents a halfway stage between the elementary Benz layout and the more modern Panhard layout. Its 9hp engine was a vertical twin-cylinder, mounted in the front of the car, and wooden artillery wheels were fitted. But the car retained the left-hand steering and other Benz-inspired features of the 1900 model.

1903 De Dion Bouton

If ever there was an automotive equivalent of Laurel and Hardy, it was the partnership of the Comte de Dion and Georges Bouton. De Dion, scion of a family that could trace its descent back to the thirteenth century, was tall, stoutly built, a pillar of society and a renowned card player and duellist: Bouton was small, lugubrious, with a vast, drooping moustache, a former locksmith's apprentice, and, until his fortuitous meeting with De Dion in 1881, a fairly unsuccessful maker of mechanical toys and model steam engines in partnership with his brother-in-law Trépardoux. It is said that Bouton and Trépardoux earned an average total of three shillings a day: even by the standards of 1880 that spelt poverty.

De Dion, a mechanical dilettante, saw one of their models, tracked them down to the wooden shed where they worked, and offered them security – a fixed income of nine shillings a day *each* – if they would come and build him a steam carriage. They agreed, and a company – De Dion, Bouton & Trépardoux – was formed. It took them two years to build their first car, a front wheel driven, rear wheel steered fourwheeler with a tall-chimneyed boiler, which was followed by limited production of a range of light steam tricycles and quadricycles, one of which won the first motor race in the world, driven by De Dion. This result was predetermined, for he was the only contestant in the event, organised by Monsieur Fossier of the *Vélocipede*, and a modest crowd turned out to watch him chuff through the suburbs of Paris in a cloud of uncondensed steam to win a somewhat hollow victory.

Later, steamers of a more substantial pattern were produced, but De Dion and Bouton were already working on the development of internal combustion engines, producing in 1889 a remarkably precocious twelve-cylinder rotary two-stroke. Piqued by their iconoclastic attitude, Trépardoux resigned. In 1895 the first successful De Dion Bouton petrol engine appeared, a tiny 0.5hp single-cylinder unit, with a bore and stroke of 50mm by 70mm. It ran at the hitherto unprecedented speed of 3000rpm on test, and was capable of 1500rpm or so in actual service without impairing its reliability.

Even the fastest engines then in service could do no more than 700–900rpm flat out: but the critics who said that the De Dion engine would not last long were confounded by the remarkable performance in competition of De Dion tricycles. Uprated versions of the De Dion engine appeared, and in 1899 a $3\frac{1}{2}$hp single-cylinder unit powered the firm's first petrol car, which had a rear engine and a two-speed transmission with the ratios engaged by expanding clutches. Of course it had a De Dion back axle, originally developed by Trépardoux for the steamers. In 1901 the car gained a $4\frac{1}{2}$hp engine and a reverse gear: the next year the famous 6hp and 8hp models, with front engines under a crocodile bonnet, made their debut.

1904 8hp Rover

J. K. Starley was the nephew of James Starley, the 'father of the cycle industry' in Coventry. He was born in 1854, and started work as a mechanic in the Ariel cycle factory in 1871, lodging with his uncle James. Around 1878 he went into business on his own account, subsequently taking into partnership William Sutton, an ex-haberdasher: later, a retired diamond merchant, George Franks, came into the firm. When, in 1883, Starley and Sutton introduced a new rear-wheel-steered tricycle on the lines of their successful Meteor model, it was Franks who evolved the name 'Rover' for it; which name soon became generally applied to the company's products. In 1885 J. K. Starley built the first successful 'safety' bicycle. The Rover Safety, with its diamond frame and equal-sized wheels, 'set the fashion to the world,' and sounded the death-knell of the high-wheeled 'ordinary' bicycle.

In 1888 the first 'Rover' car, a one-off electric three-wheeler on bath-chair lines, made its appearance, but it was not until late 1904 that Rover's first production car saw the light of day. In an era of cheap and cheerful light cars, the 8hp Rover was a design of outstanding quality and originality. The man responsible was E. W. Lewis, formerly with Daimler, who had already designed the Rover Automatic Carburetter, which was sold to motorists as a replacement fitting for their cars.

The principal feature of the Rover 8hp was its chassis construction. In fact, there was no chassis as such: engine crankcase, clutch housing, gearbox, propeller shaft housing and rear axle formed a backbone; the body was carried on a skeleton frame of ash and aluminium three-point mounted on semi-elliptic springs on the rear axle and on a transverse spring on the front axle. Aluminium was widely used throughout the car, especially in the casing of the backbone, which made the all-up weight a surprisingly low 10.5cwt, of which as much as one-eighth was represented by the engine flywheels, which were massive iron castings.

The ignition and carburetter were regulated by twist-grips set in the steering wheel rim, while the three-speed and reverse gearbox was controlled by a lever on the steering column: which was to become a feature of many American cars from the late 1930s onwards. On early models the steering column was connected to the drag links by steel cables; later, rack-and-pinion was adopted.

The 1302cc single-cylinder engine incorporated an unusual method of braking. Pressure on a special brake pedal slid the inlet and exhaust cams along the camshaft, the cams being of varying contours along their length. The first pressure on the pedal reduced the valve lift, then caused the engine to take in air through the exhaust, compress it, and release it at the top of the stroke, giving the effect of a powerful air brake.

1905 Humber

Thomas Humber began building velocipedes in his factory off the Union Road, Nottingham, in 1870, less than two years after the first bicycle had been brought into England.

Humber bicycles soon earned an enviable reputation for quality, and by 1874 the famous cycling journalist Henry Sturmey (later founder-editor of *The Autocar*) was being asked 'Why don't you get a Humber – they are the best machines out ?'

During the 1870s Humber joined forces with Thomas Rushforth Marriott, a tricyclist celebrated for having covered almost 219 miles in 24 hours, and Fred Cooper, a professional bicycle racer: shortly afterwards a large new factory was set up at Beeston, on the outskirts of Nottingham.

During the 1890s the company became involved in the vast share flotations promoted by Harry J. Lawson, a protégé of the notorious Terah Hooley, and production of motor vehicles was undertaken both at Beeston and at Coventry.

The Coventry works were responsible – guilty even – for producing a handful of improbable machines to the designs of that mechanical mountebank, E. J. Pennington, who came to England in 1896 from his native America, where his name was indissolubly linked with a hilariously unsuccessful flying machine, and with a motor bicycle said to be capable of jumping rivers. Pennington unloaded his designs on to Lawson for a cool £100,000.

Humber produced two Pennington twin-cylinder motor cycles, which were devoid of cooling system and carburetter alike, but which could run at speeds between 10 and 30mph for distances of as much as ten miles without a breakdown, and probably five Pennington Autocars, a strange 1.9-litre threewheeler with two drainpipe cylinders with a bore of 62.5mm and a stroke of no less than 305mm, with saddles for six disposed about its tubular frame and a steering system giving either driver (in the last row of the stalls) or front passenger the option of directing the machine's erratic progress. Despite a flood of orders, no Pennington machines were actually delivered to customers. Humber then took Lawson's licence to manufacture the French Léon Bollée tricar: but prototype, patterns and records were all destroyed in a fire which gutted their Coventry works, and they temporarily moved into the notorious Motor Mills, hub of the Lawson empire, where Daimler and MMC cars were already being produced.

The Company was reformed in 1900, free from the influence of Lawson, whose house-of-cards organisation was falling about his ears, and began building popular light cars, the best-known of which was the Humberette of 1903. The two factories pursued their own production policies up to 1908 – 'Beeston-Humbers' possessed more snob-appeal than 'Coventry-Humbers' – when the Nottingham works were closed down.

The 8–10hp Coventry-Humber was produced only in 1905 – it grew up into a 10–12 in 1906: the evidence of the company's years in bicycle building can be seen in its tubular frame.

1907 *TT Model Rover*

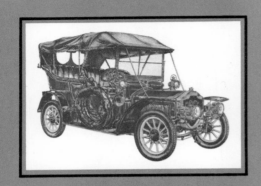

Rover's first four-cylinder car was the 16/20 of 1906, with cylinder dimensions of 95×110mm, which incorporated many features of the 8hp, such as the sliding-cam engine braking, the twist-grip controls in the rim of the steering wheel and the transverse front spring. Early examples had the steering column change, too, in which the entire outer casing of the column was rotated by the gear lever, a small metal pointer on the base of the column engaging in slots in a small quadrant behind the dash.

In 1907 two 20hps, developed from the 16/20 by boring out the engine to 97mm to give a total swept volume of 3252cc, were entered for the premier British motor sporting event, the Isle of Man Tourist Trophy. Run on May 30 over six laps of a 40½ mile circuit, the Tourist Trophy was divided into two categories, the TT proper, for which the Rovers were eligible, and the Heavy Touring Car Race, in which competitors had to fit a vertical screen like a small advertisement hoarding in the tonneau of their cars to simulate the wind resistance of a lofty limousine body.

The weather was atrocious, rain and drizzle continuing throughout the race, so E. Courtis' feat in bringing his Rover home in first place at an average speed of 28.8mph was quite remarkable. Moreover, he had beaten the time of the winner of the Heavy Touring Car Race, the well-known former racing cyclist George Pilkington Mills, driving a Beeston-Humber.

Three weeks after the race Rover unveiled what must have been one of the first 'catalogue competition cars,' the 20hp Tourist Trophy Model, which differed from the racer in having a longer wheelbase and wooden artillery, rather than wire, wheels.

A new design of radiator was fitted, which incorporated the shield-shape used in the name-plates of the 'Imperial' Rover cycles and motor cycles. The old transverse front spring was retained, but its mountings were strengthened to 'present a massive and workmanlike appearance.'

The pressed steel scuttle incorporated the petrol tank, which fed the carburetter – Rover Automatic, of course! – by gravity. The cylinders were cast separately, and the rearmost one nestled cosily beneath the petrol tank, although this did not impair accessibility too much.

A four-speed gearbox with overdrive top was standard, in which form the car was capable of 45mph and cost £450 with four seated rotund phaeton coachwork: a three-speed version, of which an example is preserved by the Rover Company, was £50 cheaper.

In an interview, J. K. Starley said that 'the Tourist Trophy conditions had, at any rate in the case of his company, evolved a car which they could supply and put before the public with the utmost confidence that it was a real touring car in every respect, and not one specially designed to run in competition, and never be heard of as a standard car afterwards.'

1907 Rover

The revolutionary 'chassisless' construction of the original 8hp Rover of 1904 quickly fell victim to orthodoxy: it was replaced by an ash chassis strengthened with steel flitch-plates, and more conventional suspension. However, such features as the steering column gearchange and the sliding cam engine brake were retained.

It was on one of these redesigned 8hp models that Robert L. Jefferson proposed to drive from Coventry to Istanbul in 1905. This project meant that Jefferson would go where no motorist had ever penetrated: indeed, the trans-European journey had only once before been attempted, by one Doctor Lehwess, sometime racing motorist, who had set off from London in a vast 25hp Panhard-Levassor motor caravan named 'Passe Partout' accompanied by an Argyll voiturette as tender car to circumnavigate the earth.

Dr Lehwess and his companions wined and dined their way across Europe in a leisurely fashion, selling souvenir postcards to defray their expenses. The trip ended in a fiasco, with the 'Passe Partout' stuck fast in a glutinous snow-covered mudhole near Nijni Novgorod, in Eastern Russia: Lehwess and Co went home by train.

Jefferson planned a more strenuous route than Lehwess: his course lay across the Balkans, where roads were few and cut-throats plentiful. The Rover was specially modified for the journey, with a box body, such as was later to become popular with commercial travellers for the carriage of samples. In this case, spares and provisions were stored under the seats. As passenger, Jefferson carried Robert Weallans, chief test driver of Rover.

The trip across Europe was, to begin with, relatively devoid of trouble. True, there were the usual obstructive minor officials who did their best to impede the car's progress: but it only took Jefferson five weeks to reach Belgrade. This was where his troubles were really to start, for he was now faced with the ascent of the Balkans, a feat hitherto unachieved by a motorcar.

The track over the mountains was rutted, flanked by sheer drops, and had an average gradient of 1:4. Moreover, it was one long succession of hairpin bends, and the motorists had continually to dismount and move boulders out of the way.

But they were successful in making the ascent, which was followed by an equally hair raising down-grade into Bulgaria. Jefferson nearly caused a diplomatic row by running through the Bulgarian customs post without stopping, but was suffered to proceed.

The last stretch of the run was slow and trying, with Weallans performing marvels of ingenuity in repairing the damage after the car had turned over in mid-Roumelia.

Despite this, and other incidents, Jefferson succeeded in reaching Istanbul, forty-five days after he had set off.

1908 Riley Tourer 12/18

'Old Midnight' was what the employees at the Riley Cycle Company of Coventry christened their prototype 12–18hp model, introduced at the 1907 Olympia Exhibition, because its development had entailed so much overtime working.

The 12-18 was designed by the brothers Percy and Stanley Riley: Percy had constructed his first motor car in 1896–8, having just left grammar school. He hand-filed the gears for this little voiturette himself, and fitted its single-cylinder engine with one of the earliest examples of a mechanically-operated inlet valve: most early cars breathed through automatic inlets, in which the suck of the piston pulled open the valve against the pressure of a light spring.

The 12-18 was the logical successor to Riley's first production four-wheeler, the 9hp of 1906, which followed a line of tricars of more or less motor cycle type. Like the 9hp, the 12-18 had a vee-twin engine and a constant-mesh gearbox, with the ratios selected by dog-clutches. In an era when few drivers could change gear on a conventional gearbox without a horrendous 'sidegrubbing of teeth', the silence and ease of the Riley change met with a good deal of favourable comment. Novel, too, was the use of detachable wheels: most cars had fixed wheels, which meant that the frequent punctures had to be dealt with in situ. Riley used their own design of detachable wheel, which was subsequently adopted by a number of other manufacturers: the 9hp was said to have been the first car to feature detachable wheels as a standard item of equipment.

The engine of the 12-18 had a bore of 102mm and a stroke of 127mm, giving a swept volume of 2113cc: it had a fairly effective system of pump-fed lubrication, fed from an oil tank under the bonnet. For its engine capacity, the 12-18 was no mean performer for its day: in May 1908 a four-seated example achieved 48mph over a flying kilometre on the private speed course on the Duke of Portland's estate at Welbeck Abbey, and a similar model won the Ballinaslaughter Hill Climb and made a virtual non-stop run in the Irish Reliability Trials of 1908.

The 12-18 was available with either 'short' or 'long' chassis. The former sold for 225 guineas in two-seater and 235 guineas in four-seater form, and had an 8ft wheelbase. The 'long' with a 9ft wheelbase, cost £283 with five-seated 'rotund' coachwork.

With their ovoid radiator and well-designed bodywork, the 12-18 Riley and its smaller sibling, the 10hp, introduced for 1908, were among the more handsome light cars of their day, and really laid the foundations for Riley's reputation as makers of high-quality cars of moderate capacity. It is difficult to see in them the genesis of the successful and much-loved Riley Nine of 1927—which did so much to establish the image of the high-performance, economical light car: but the same designers were responsible for the later model, too.

1909 Maudslay 17hp

There was almost a hundred years of engineering experience behind the Maudslay Motor Company when it was founded in 1902 as an offshoot of the business founded by the celebrated engineer Henry Maudslay, whose discoveries – such as the screw-cutting lathe – had done much to pave the way for the development of the motor car. Maudslay marine engines had been made since 1815, when the prototype powered the paddle-steamer *Richmond*, the first steamboat to ply on the Thames, and had included the gigantic four-cylinder power unit for Brunel's *Great Eastern*, which had bores of 1900mm and strokes of 4200mm approximately.

So it was only to be expected that the Maudslay car was something out of the ordinary. Quite apart from its beautiful finish, the Maudslay was the first production car to feature an overhead camshaft. Mind you, Maudslay didn't really appreciate the benefits this layout could provide in terms of extra engine power: they adopted it because it made the valves more accessible when they needed attention, and, indeed, the original 1902 model had atmospherically-operated inlet valves. Within twelve months however, Maudslay were stating: 'Our 1903 type of motor is fitted with mechanically operated valves, improved fan-cooled radiator, and many other minor improvements.'

The bevel-driven camshaft was carried in a special mounting, bolted on one side of the cylinders and hinged on the other, which could be swung back to permit work on the valves without upsetting their timing.

The original model was a 20hp three-cylinder – several leading makers, including Rolls-Royce and Panhard, included threes in their range because of their excellent balance. Unusually for its date, the 20hp Maudslay had considerably oversquare cylinders – the actual figures were 114×100mm – and was notably smooth-running.

The most common coachwork on the 20hp was a 'Waggonette Omnibus,' which had a detachable 'hard top' over the rear seats, with plate-glass windows fitted with roller blinds, which could be hoisted up into the roof of the coach-house when not required.

Four and six-cylinder models were dropped in 1906, and production concentrated on fours, which by now had acquired handsome circular radiators and bonnets, an eccentricity which they had in common with another famous firm of marine engineers, Delaunay-Belleville.

By 1912 the range had been reduced to two, the 90×130mm four-cylinder 'Sweet Seventeen,' originally introduced for the 1910 season and priced at £425 in chassis form, and the 27hp six, with identical cylinder dimensions: both had silent all-chain gearboxes with the ratios selected by dog-clutches.

1910 7hp Swift

'A Good Small Car' is how the Swift Motor Company referred to their new 7hp model in their 1910 catalogue, adding: 'Many would commence motoring if only assured of a good car at or about £150. Price difficulty no longer exists, for it is now possible to obtain a car embodying the highest standard in design combined with the best material and workmanship at the moderate price of £147 complete. This car is the latest 7hp single cylinder SWIFT. The production of this car has been based on nine years' actual manufacturing experience of good, reliable cars. Exhaustive tests have been carried out, so that to-day we are in a position to recommend this car with the utmost confidence, for it is not only soundly constructed and thoroughly reliable, but it is inexpensive to run and maintain.'

From which you might consider that Swift had burnt much midnight oil in designing this long-awaited economy model: but such was hardly the case, since the sum total of their labours lay in the fitting of their own pattern of radiator, for the 7hp was somewhat of a cuckoo in the Swift's nest. It was in fact an automotive case of 'the Colonel's lady and Judy O'Grady,' for the 7hp chassis was built by Austin in their Longbridge, Birmingham factory, and sold by them as the 7hp Austin, but without the same enthusiasm, apparently, as Swift promoted its 'sister under the skin.'

Even by the standards of 1910 the single-cylinder Swift was hopelessly outmoded, with its rough engine of one-chuff-per-telegraph pole type and its ill-chosen gear ratios: and it was out of production by 1913, when it was supplanted by a much nicer twin-cylinder 7hp cyclecar.

Not that the 1910 7hp was the first bad car to bear the Swift nameplate. Originally makers of 'Swiftsure' sewing machines, the company had been the first (under its original title of European Sewing Machine Company, later Coventry Machinists' Company) to produce bicycles in England, in 1869, originally making boneshakers and in 1870, to the designs of James Starley, the first 'ordinary' or 'penny-farthing' bicycle.

Their first foray into the world of car manufacture had taken the form of a 4½hp MMC-powered voiturette, with an unsprung back axle and an unusual form of gearchange in which there were two sets of teeth on the crown wheel and two pinions, the choice of ratio being determined by dog clutch. To start this mechanical masterpiece the crankhandle was inserted into an aperture on the back axle. The probability of trouble with this layout, even to the uncritical eyes of the motorist of 1902, was far from encouraging.

1911 Daimler

The Daimler Motor Company of Coventry was originally part of Harry Lawson's grandiose empire, and was floated by him in January 1896 to exploit the British rights to Gottleib Daimler's patents in England. Though they used Daimler narrow-V-twin engines, the cars they built were rather blacksmithed versions of the contemporary Panhard-Levassors. They shared the Coventry Motor Mills with another of Lawson's companies, the Motor Manufacturing Company (*né* the Great Horseless Carriage Company), who occupied the bulk of the building. Daimler had a vast signboard right across the front of the building but, as I was told by a former MMC employee, Daimler 'only occupied the sheds round the back.'

Be that as it may, there was precious little difference between Daimler and MMC cars in the early days – apparently Daimler made the chassis and MMC the coachwork, and in most cases only the manufacturer's nameplate indicated the make.

One of the earliest Daimler cars was driven from John O'Groats to Land's End in October 1897 by J. J. Henry Sturmey, first editor of *The Autocar* and a director of Daimler to boot. It took seventeen days to cover the 939 miles, at an average running speed of just under 10mph, consuming 67.5 gallons of fuel: and having reached Land's End, Sturmey turned round and drove back to Coventry, making the total mileage for the journey exactly 1600.

After Lawson's empire collapsed Daimler were reformed in 1904; the cars were developed from crude, fast chain-driven machines into reasonably refined live-axle transmission cars under the aegis of Dr F. W. Lanchester, who had resigned from the company bearing his name to act as Consulting Engineer to Daimler.

Then Daimler were visited by a persuasive American demonstrating a chassis powered by a new kind of 'valveless' engine he had invented, which he claimed was completely silent. Even the brake rods of the chassis were swathed in flannel to prevent them rattling. The American was Charles Yale Knight: so the 'valveless' engine he had designed was known as the Silent Knight. In fact, the cylinder was virtually all-valve, the space between the cylinder walls and the piston being taken up by two concentric sleeves moved up and down by eccentrics on a camshaft: slots in these sleeves coincided at appropriate points to allow petrol/air mixture in and exhaust gases out. The only trouble was that the engine, even when only moderately worn, consumed vast quantities of oil, even after Lanchester had done his best with it. But Daimler persisted with a vast range of sleeve valves until the 1930s: King George V was an enthusiastic customer.

1911 Austin Town Carriage

The height of elegance in Edwardian society was to have a car especially for town work and social calls: in America electromobiles were popular, but in England they tended to prove expensive and inconvenient, as there were not the ready sources of cheap electricity available that there were in the USA.

However, British society valued the 'bonnetless' look, which gave the appearance of an electric by hiding the engine under the chauffeur's seat: this may have made the chauffeur uncomfortable in hot weather, but then he was paid £3 a week to put up with such inconveniences. Thus, a typical owner's terms of 1906 ran:'Whenever I want the car, it and you must be ready. You may have to stay up all night getting it ready: I want to know nothing about that, all I care about is that it should always be ready and in good condition – which means that whenever it comes in you must not leave it until it is cleaned, washed, filled and ready for the road. You may expect a whole day off every week, and you will often not be required for days at a time; but you must always be ready. If not, it will be understood that you have failed in the performance of your duties, and that you go.'

'Any good man will cheerfully accept such terms,' he concluded.

One of the last of the bonnetless cars was the 15hp Austin Ladies' Town Landaulette introduced in 1909, and based on the chassis of the 1908 12cwt Austin commercial, designed to take delivery van, commercial traveller's brougham or public service vehicle bodywork.

The main feature of the Ladies' Town Landaulette was the central placing of the driver's seat, which gave him 'a clear view from either side to rearwards.'

In fact, this massive-looking vehicle was only 11 feet long overall: but its appearance suggested the apocalyptic Holy City in that the length and the height and the breadth of it appeared equal. Also typical of town carriage design was the brass speaking trumpet conveniently placed behind the chauffeur's right ear. If he failed to respond to instructions from the trumpet, then a sharp jab in the back of the neck from an elegant parasol poked through the brass-rimmed Hall's Motor Communicator in the front window of the rear compartment would attract his attention rather more forcibly!

A normally-bonnetted version of the 15hp was also available: in 1910 Miss Vera Holm acted as chauffeuse to the suffragette leader Mrs Pankhurst on such a car on a tour of Scotland.

1912 Rover Landaulet

In 1909 Rover, like so many quality car makers, had fallen for the fashionable vogue for the Silent Knight engine, and from then on their range became more and more dominated by lethargic sleeve-valve motorcars. There was even an 8hp single-cylinder model of just over a litre capacity, which must have been the ultimate in sluggishness.

Fortunately, in 1911 Rover took on a new chief designer, Owen Clegg, formerly of Wolseley. Clegg laid down a conventional four-cylinder poppet-valve car, of notably clean lines and beautifully finished.

Clegg's new model was known as the Rover Twelve, although the engine was actually of 13.9hp by the Royal Automobile Club's rating, having engine dimensions of 75×130mm, and a swept volume of 2297cc. The engine was a particularly advanced piece of foundry work, being a monobloc casting of smooth exterior lines, featuring ample water passages round the cylinders. In fact, just about everything that could be water-jacketed was, for both inlet and exhaust manifolds were cast into the block, and surrounded by water, and the carburetter – an SU built under Rover licence – was also water-cooled. The cylinder head was cast in unit with the block, and it has been said of the engine that it was 'a unit of such clean lines that it looked almost like a two-stroke.'

The engine was designed for smooth running, with a désaxé crankshaft carried in three main bearings, copiously lubricated by pump and splash. The transmission was designed for silence, too, with an underslung worm driving the rear axle. The car was intended for the new and rising class of owner-drivers: it proved an instant success, and soon represented Rover's entire output. The company was now entirely self-sufficient, possessing its own foundry and coachbuilding shops, whence emanated two-seated and four-seated touring bodies, coupés and landaulettes for the Twelves. The car found especial favour with those critical customers, the doctors.

Clegg had advanced ideas on production techniques, and laid down cars in batches in a tentative form of mass-production. From a dozen or so cars at one time, the batches grew to five hundred. Electric lighting was soon standardised, and for its price of £350 the Rover represented amazing value for money. The company's claim that it was 'acknowledged by all, Clients and Competitors alike, to be the Finest Car in the World' was not without foundation.

However, during the Great War the company failed to gain a contract to build staff cars, and made 16hp Sunbeams under licence instead. The Twelve was revived after the Armistice – in updated form it survived until 1924.

1912 Benz Grand Tourer

It was only seven years after Benz had abandoned their archaic rear-engined cars, little changed from Karl Benz' 1894 Vélo and recognisably descended from his 1885 threewheeler, that they introduced the 21.5 litre Blitzen Benz racing car. It was developed from the relatively diminutive (!) Grand Prix Benz of 1908 which had a swept volume of 15 litres, and had a similar engine bored out to give cylinder dimensions of 185×200mm: with each Wagnerian heave of its four 7¼in diameter pistons the Benz chuffed over 5 litres of exhaust gas down its stove-pipe-sized tailpipe.

The overhead valves, one inlet, one exhaust, per cylinder, were operated by exposed pushrods. It was easy enough to remove the exhaust valves when they needed attention by removing the inlet valve cages, freeing the exhaust valves and letting them drop into the cylinder, then putting one's hand into the inlet port and drawing the valve out. While the inlet pipe was of Brobdignagian proportions, only one carburetter supplied the engine's gaseous requirements. It can't have been that short of breath, however, for in 1909 a Blitzen Benz set up a world speed record of 127.4mph at Brooklands, increased this to 131.1mph on Daytona Beach in 1910, and reached 141.7mph the following year.

Leading American drivers such as the cigar-chomping Barney Oldfield and Bob Burman favoured the Blitzen Benz in their barn-storming careers: at every county fair where the attendance figures justified his presence, Oldfield would broadside round the dirt-surfaced trotting track to shatter convincingly the local 'record' for the benefit of the open-mouthed spectators.

At Brooklands L. G. 'Cupid' Hornsted had graduated from a 150hp racer to a 200hp short wheelbase 'Big Black Benz,' which was geared to give 140mph at 1400rpm in top gear when the tyres stood the strain. Even the best racing tyres then available, Palmer Cords, only lasted 58.5 miles: other makes burst after 20.

On one occasion a tyre burst when Hornsted was going for an hour record, jamming a driving chain; the car spun round, shot off the track and landed in the notorious Brooklands sewage farm, fortunately without major injury to its occupants.

In 1913 Benz introduced a touring car with a Blitzen-type engine which retailed at £1800, by far the largest-engined motorcar ever catalogued for sale to the public. During the Great War, high-ranking German officers used 200hp Benz as staff transport: the car pictured here is said to have belonged to Field-Marshal von Hindenburg.

1912 Crouch Carette 8hp

One of the stranger phenomena of motoring history was the sudden genesis of the 'Motoring for the Million' movement in the 1910–12 period. Pioneered by Morgan in England and Bourbeau & Devaux in France, tiny companies began building 'cyclecars' of varying degrees of crudity. The name 'cyclecar' derived from the widespread use of motor cycle techniques in the manufacture of these ultra-cheap vehicles: the use of tubular frames, vee-twin engines and belt or chain final-drive. The general philosophy behind these little three- and four-wheeled cars was that the type of customer who would be able to afford them because of their modest price would either be an impecunious family man seeking cheap transport, who would be sufficiently unversed in motor mechanics to overlook the major shortcomings in the design of his first vehicle, or would be a motor cyclist looking for a mount of suitably sporting proclivities in which he could transport his lady friends in moderate comfort, and who viewed the driving of a more or less lethal bolide as a challenge to his virility.

In both cases, the customers were pleased most of the time—at least until low-priced 'real' cars such as the Bébé Peugeot (designed by Ettore Bugatti), the Singer 10 and the 9hp AC began to appear.

One of the earlier exponents of the art of cyclecar manufacture in Britain was the Crouch Motor Company, of Tower Gate Works, Cook Street, Coventry, whose three-wheeled Carette appeared at the height of the 'new motoring' boom in 1912.

The Carette had a vee-twin Coventry-Simplex engine, rated at 7.9hp, with a bore and stroke of 80×90mm, making the cubic capacity 1-litre. The engine was centrally mounted in the chassis, a position becoming fashionable nowadays for sports-racing cars. But there was no thought of improved weight distribution or handling behind the mid-mounting of the Crouch power unit: it was done simply to give as short a distance as possible between crankshaft, gearbox and back wheel to give the driving chains an easier life. Although a short bonnet was fitted, its sole purpose was to keep the lower extremities of the driver and passenger dry: with the radiator mounted only an inch or so in front of the pedals, the driver could hardly have complained of cold feet. Complete, the Crouch Carette cost £110: a four-wheeled version, introduced soon after the three-wheeler, cost £128.

The three-wheeler was revived after the war, priced at a modest (for 1919!) £260: it was succeeded in 1923 by a more conventional, front-engined car, still with a vee-twin power unit. A four-cylinder engine soon followed.

1912 *Turner 10hp*

Although the Belgian motor industry today confines its activities to the assembly of imported parts, there was a time when Belgian – designed and built cars were a force to be reckoned with. The Minerva, the Excelsior and the Métallurgique were among the finest cars of the decade 1904–14, and even at an earlier date, Belgian designs were highly regarded.

Thus Burford & Van Toll, of Twickenham, acquired the licence to build Belgian Vivinus voiturettes in England in 1900, while a couple of years later the Wolverhampton firm of Thomas Turner & Co started to import Miesse steam cars from Brussels; in 1904 they began the actual manufacture of these vehicles under the name Turner-Miesse.

The basic design of the Miesse dated back to 1896: production had begun in earnest in 1898. The cars had three-cylinder engines which were single-acting—the steam was only admitted above the piston, unlike double-acting engines, where steam pushed the piston in both directions—and which were supplied from a flash generator of the type pioneered by the Frenchman Léon Serpollet, in which small quantities of water were pumped into a tubular generator heated by a paraffin burner.

As the water came into contact with the hot metal, it was instantly 'flashed' into dry, superheated steam. The care, maintenance and driving of steam cars tended to be more complex than on petrol cars, and Miesse had abandoned their steam designs by 1907.

Not so Turner, however, for they continued to make steam cars on Miesse lines right up to 1913, when a range of five models, from 10 to 30hp was marketed, at prices ranging from £250 to £650. In 1907 Turners briefly essayed a petrol car, the 20–25hp Seymour-Turner, built for the big motor retailing company of Seymours Ltd, of Brompton Road, Kensington, which retailed at £450 in chassis form. It was five years before they tried another petrol-engined model.

In 1911 the 9hp vee-twin Turner light car appeared. This was uprated to 10hp in 1912, when two four-cylinder models were added to the range. There was a 15hp, 75 × 120mm car, with the cylinders cast in a single block, which had a three-speed gearbox and cost £365 complete with four-seater body and cape cart hood, and a little 10hp model, with a similar chassis and body to the twin-cylinder car, with a two-speed gear and worm final drive. The cost of the extra two cylinders was high: the vee-twin sold for £165 complete, while the four was priced between £197 and £222, dependent on how well finished the coachwork was.

With the passing of the steam cars, the little 10hp became Turners' staple offering: it acquired a three-speed gearbox, (four speeds on the sporting variant), and was also marketed under the JB and Universal labels.

1913 Swift 7hp

'The one thing that was needed to complete Motor History' was how Swift trumpeted the introduction of their new 7hp twin-cylinder cyclecar at the 1912 Motor Cycle & Cyclecar Exhibition at Olympia. It wasn't that wonderful a car, although it was a vast improvement on the 7hp single that had preceded it.

The engine was a vertical twin of 75×110mm, with a swept volume of 972cc, and a petrol consumption in the region of 35mpg. Lubrication was by guess or by God, the oil being drip fed from a tank under the bonnet through a sight glass on the dashboard, and there was a proper three-speed and reverse gearbox and bevel-drive back axle.

The chassis construction reflected the company's 'roots in the cycle industry, for it was tubular, with lugs fitted to carry the cross-members. It was also not particularly strong – one surviving example of this model has had a secondary chassis frame added to stop the car from folding in the middle – and was replaced in 1914 by a more up-to-date pressed steel chassis.

At the same time that the chassis was altered, the steering was modified. The original model had rack-and-pinion steering giving half-a-turn lock-to-lock: later models had directional control by geared-down worm-and-sector. Although rack-and-pinion steering is made so much of as a 'quality' feature on modern cars, it is salutary to recall that until quite recently it was only considered fit for use on the very cheapest vehicles; indeed, it was thought of as virtually on a par with the dreaded cable-and-bobbin which graced (or disgraced?) the crudest of the cyclecars of the 1910-20 era.

Alongside the 7hp Swift marketed an unnecessarily large range of more conventional fours, a 65×100mm 10hp, a 69×120mm 11.9hp, a 75×110mm 14hp, an 80×130mm 15.9hp and a 90×120mm 20hp.

The Armistice saw this uneconomic list pruned drastically: only an updated 12hp was shown at the 1919 Motor Exhibition, to be joined soon after by a new 10hp model.

For 1926 two new models, yet another 10hp and a 12/35hp, of 1097cc and 1954cc respectively, were introduced: these were the first Swifts to feature four-wheel brakes; the next year, although its engine remained unchanged, the 12/35 became a 14/40hp, the latter being a rather fashionable horsepower rating adopted by several of the more popular middle-class makers such as Vauxhall, Bean and Star.

Fashionable or not, Swift were finding the going hard, not having sufficient capital to complete with other manufacturers who could afford to cut prices to attract customers: Swift had to put their prices up, and 1928 saw them offering only an improved 10hp with a four-speed gearbox replacing the three-speed unit of the earlier model. By 1932 the marque was dead.

1913 *Arden*

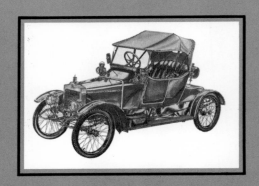

In 1912, a builder named Isherwood, from Balsall Common, Berkswell, near Coventry, decided like so many others at that time, that there was a big future for the small car, and went into motor manufacture for the masses, calling his cars 'Arden'.

The first Arden was a fairly crude two-seater with an air-cooled vee-twin JAP engine of 85×85mm bore and stroke. The chassis design was about ten years out of date, the main members being of oak strengthened with steel flitch plates. The front suspension was by three-quarter-elliptic springs, a pattern which Mercedes had abandoned due to their unfortunate effect on handling: but their advantage for a cheap car such as the Arden was that they could be bolted on to the front of a basic rectangular chassis without the need for separate dumb-irons. Rear suspension was more conventional, with semi-elliptic springs. Originally, the Arden had cable and bobbin steering, but as it became more of a true light car, this layout was abandoned in favour of the more conventional (and less suicidal) worm and sector. Unusually for such a cheap car (£115 without hood and windscreen, which cost another seven guineas), a proper three-speed and reverse gearbox was fitted.

In late 1913 a water-cooled version was introduced. This had a vertical twin Alpha engine, a neat proprietary sidevalve power unit with a bore and stroke of 85×95mm, and a capacity of 1092cc. Lubrication, like much of the rest of the design of this car, was well behind the times. A gallon oil tank on the dashboard was equipped with a handpump: this fed oil through a sight glass, to drip or splash on to the engine bearings, the principle adopted being to adjust the flow so that a blue haze of oil smoke was just apparent in the exhaust. This system of oiling was found on motor-cycles and cheap cars at this period: a similar layout, but with a mechanical oil pump, survived on Morgan three-wheelers right through the 1920s.

The extra cost of the water-cooling, with its handsome brass radiator, brought the price of the Arden up to £145.

There was also a £160 four-cylinder Arden on the market in 1914 with a 59×100mm engine of around 1100cc, powerful enough to pull three- and four-seated coachwork. Arden built probably a couple of hundred cars in all before war broke out. Production then ceased as the company went over to making munitions.

But that wasn't quite the end of the story. In 1920 the Alpha engine company was acquired by Ransomes, Simms & Jefferies, who used the twin-cylinder Alpha engines in their larger motor lawn mowers right up until the outbreak of the Second World War.

1913 GWK

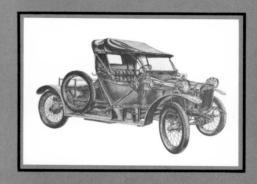

'A Gear for Every Gradient' was the claim made by Messrs Grice, Wood & Keiller for the infinitely variable transmission fitted to their GWK light car, which had first appeared in 1910. This transmission, reputedly derived by Grice from the mechanism of a machine used for grinding optical lenses, worked by friction. A flat face was machined on the engine flywheel, where conventional transmissions would have had the clutch. At right angles to this surface was a wheel, with a friction band around its periphery, rubbing on the flywheel.

Depressing the clutch pedal moved this friction disc out of contact with the flywheel, and the driver selected a 'gear' with a lever, which moved the disc towards the outer rim of the flywheel for a high gear or inwards for a low gear, it being obvious that the speed of rotation at various points on the radius decreased the nearer the centre of the flywheel was approached. In fact the centre was dished to give the effect of a neutral: moving the friction disc to the other side of this neutral area gave a choice of reverse ratios.

The GWK had an early form of two-pedal control: depressing the clutch pedal fully brought a transmission brake into play. It should be noted that if the 'gear change' was made too hurriedly, a flat spot was worn on the friction facing, which then set up a rhythmic thumping noise as the car travelled along: but the facing material – compressed paper at first, and later cork – was cheap and easy to replace, and many owners thought it worth the bother to escape from the embarrassment of a bungled change on a conventional sliding-cog gearbox.

At £150 fully equipped the GWK represented good value for money, and was relatively fast, 55mph being obtainable. The original model had a 9.2hp, 1069cc, vertical twin side-valve engine set transversely across the frame immediately behind the driver's seat: this power unit was supplied by Coventry-Simplex, who were to become Coventry Climax in 1917.

Unusually for such a low-priced car, the GWK had a proper pressed-steel-frame with semi-elliptic front, quarter-elliptic rear springing – most cheap cars of the period had tubular frames and quarter-elliptic springs all round.

In the period from 1911, when production began, in a little factory at Datchet, Buckinghamshire, to 1915, when the company turned its attention to wartime Admiralty contracts, over 1000 9.2hp GWKs were sold.

A postwar attempt to produce a four-cylinder version, powered by a 10.8hp 1368cc Coventry Climax engine, in a new factory, the Cordwalles works at Maidenhead, proved unsuccessful. The company even tried to build 'new' rear-engined 9.2hp cars from pre-war spares, but to no avail, and after several financial crises they went out of business in 1930, and Mr Keiller went over to marmalade making in the Maidenhead factory.

1913 Morris-Oxford

William Morris had established himself as a cycle maker and repairer in the Oxford suburb of Cowley at the age of 16 in 1893. Morris gained much publicity for his machines with his successes in track racing, and within a short space of time his sales figures had risen sufficiently to enable him to move out of the shed behind his father's house, where he had started production, into a proper shop in High Street, Oxford.

In 1901 he began building motor cycles, which led him into the motor trade: his 'Morris Garage' motor agency at Longwall, Oxford, expanded rapidly, soon acquiring the title of 'The Oxford Motor Palace,' and the cycle and motor cycle side of the business was sold off.

Morris really represented the advent of the motor age in Oxford, and his red motor omnibuses were notorious throughout the city. In fact, so successful did he become that he decided to go into production of a light car to meet the growing demand for a moderately priced motor for the middle-class owner-driver.

Finance was a problem, and Morris decided that the surest answer to the question lay in buying components ready-made from outside suppliers: a disused military college in Cowley was acquired, and late 1912 the first Morris-Oxford light car was under construction.

Unlike the crude cyclecars that were enjoying a brief boom at that time, the Morris-Oxford was an utterly conventional 'big car in miniature'. It had a specially-built White & Poppe engine of 1018cc swept volume, a neat little sidevalve power-plant with a three-speed gearbox built in unit — at that period most cars had separate engine and gearbox — and a worm-drive rear axle.

Priced at £175 complete, the Morris-Oxford made its public debut at the North of England Motor Show in February 1913: but the prototype engine had not been built, and a wooden dummy was fitted in its place.

The body on the Morris was nominally a two-seater, but since William Morris was a notably slim man, only the thinnest could comfortably sit abreast: a slightly larger De Luxe model, with the track widened by 5in to 3ft 9in, and the wheelbase of 7ft extended to 7ft 6in was introduced at the end of 1913, at a cost completely equipped of £199 10s.

While the Morris-Oxford was a lively performer for those days, with a top speed of 55mph in standard form, it was prone to overheating, even though its rounded radiator was quite generously proportioned. The Fivet-engined 10hp AC, the Morris' closest rival, had a similar radiator, and when I drove the sole survivor of this model, the AC showed no tendency to boil. But the Morris, soon to acquire the nickname 'Bullnose' — which was colloquially used as a term of opprobrium at the time — boiled spectacularly and often.

1921 Rover 8hp

'Unaffected by frost or by heat, accessible to a degree, fool-proof and cheap to make and replace, the 8hp car is one which can be easily understood by the most inexperienced motorist and in case of accident can be put right not only by the large garages in the cities, but by any average motor cycle agent anywhere.' Such was the long-winded preamble with which Rover introduced their 8hp flat-twin economy model, which they had brought out in 1919 to meet the tremendous demand for cheap motorcars, for transport at a reasonable price for the thousands of ex-soldiers who had first sampled the internal combustion engine in the War.

Many post-war economy cars were crude in conception and execution, and positively unsafe on the road: but the little Rover was well-made considering its low price (£220) even if the coachwork was somewhat uncouth.

The engine owed more to contemporary motor cycle design than to car practice, with its two well-finned 85x85mm cylinders sticking out through the sides of the stubby bonnet under protruberant air scoops, which were intended to augment the somewhat haphazard cooling arrangements. When labouring uphill, the car not unnaturally tended to overheat, although stories of the cylinder heads glowing cherry red are doubtless unfounded.

The chassis was as basic as could be, merely a channel steel rectangle with minimal cross-bracing, and quarter-elliptic springs bolted on at each corner.

A three-speed gearbox was mounted in unit with the engine, controlled by a long, wavery poker of a gear-lever such as was not to deface the generality of motorcars for a decade to come.

Accessibility was quite a strong point of the design, although if reports of the unreliability of early models are to be believed, the cylinder heads were prone to detach themselves unaided in moments of stress. One cunning feature was that the nameplate on the dummy radiator could quickly be removed to enable the magneto to be adjusted without removing the bonnet.

At first, the standard coachwork was an open two-seater, with a capacious luggage boot, but later on other versions, such as a three-seater, a four-seated tourer or a commercial traveller's car were added to the range.

Quite the most luxurious of the Rover 8s was the coupé, an example of which carried off a silver medal in the 1923 Scottish Six Day's Trial. By 1923, indeed, over 10,000 Rover 8s of all types had been sold, but the model's days were numbered, despite an increase in engine capacity to give more power. By 1925 it had been replaced by a more conventional, more expensive 9/20hp four cylinder car.

1921 10/30 Alvis

If you enter the tiny museum in the Dorset village of Corfe Castle, you will be confronted by the rusty remains of what was once a singularly unlovely front-wheel-driven motorscooter of 1919 vintage, fitted with a 211cc Minerva engine of much earlier date.

This crude contrivance was the first motor vehicle to be produced by T. G. John Ltd, of Coventry: surprisingly, the company's next venture was a high-quality light car, 'luxurious and super-efficient in every detail', which it would have to have been to justify its basic price tag of £685, even in the car-hungry boom conditions of 1920, for this was twice as much as most cars of similar engine capacity cost. The new car was called the 'Alvis', the name being originally coined by its designer, G. P. H. de Freville, for his patent aluminium pistons produced for World War One aeroengines.

The Alvis was one of the earliest British production cars to be fitted with aluminium pistons in place of the then universal cast iron or steel type, although British engineers had pioneered their use before the war. In 1912 Professor A. M. Low, one of the most brilliant and prolific designers of the 1910–20 era, whose inherent dilettantism caused many of his discoveries to go disregarded, fitted his Gregoire car with aluminium pistons, this being the first substantiable record of their use. The next year W. O. Bentley persuaded the French company DFP, whose British concessionaire he was, to fit aluminium pistons in the interests of speed.

The effect of aluminium pistons on the Alvis was that the engine, an otherwise orthodox sidevalve unit of 1498cc, developed over 30bhp at 3500rpm, a high output for such a small engine at that date.

The two-seater version had a novel form of body construction developed by Morgans of Long Acre, and first shown by them fitted to a Crossley at the 1919 Motor Show. 'This construction', claimed Morgan, 'can be carried out to any design at half the weight with twice the strength of any other model.' The secret of the construction was that it was based on contemporary aircraft practice. A light tubular steel framework was braced with straining wires and turnbuckles: sheet aluminium panelling was laid over this; the Alvis body weighed less than 1.5cwt complete, and the entire car weighed only 14cwt ready for the road.

The 1921 car illustrated here has this type of coachwork, and is the oldest known Alvis. It features the original pattern of radiator badge, a winged triangle bearing the name 'Alvis': it transpired that this infringed the trade mark of the Avro aeroplane company, and during 1921 this was changed for the inverted triangle badge which Alvis cars bore until the end of production in 1967.

In 1921 a new overhead valve 1598cc model, the 11/40 appeared, then in 1923 the 10/30, too, acquired ohv and pointed-tail sports aluminium coachwork: the engine dimensions were quickly altered from 65×110mm to 68×103mm (1496cc) and the well loved 12/50 Alvis was born. 'It is a road car de luxe such as I did not expect to see for ten years to come', commented B. H. Davies, 'Runabout' of *The Autocar*.

1924 Stoneleigh 9hp

Armstrong Siddeley Motors were formed in 1919 by the fusion of the car manufacturing interests of the Sir W. G. Armstrong, Whitworth Company and Siddeley-Deasy, starting production with a massively-built 30hp four.

Although the car had overhead valves, no attempt was made to give it high-speed performance: rather, it was intended as a durable car for the upper-middle-class market, and its styling was obviously not intended to go out of date in a hurry. The car was distinguished by an almost monolithic vee-radiator surmounted by a crouching Sphinx mascot and multi-stud pressed-steel disc wheels.

Although Armstrong Siddeley billed their product as 'cars of aircraft quality', there was nothing light or streamlined about them. To produce a cheap light car for the masses hardly seemed in character: so when, in 1922, Armstrong Siddeley took this unlikely step, they disguised the end-product under the name 'Stoneleigh', a name that had already been used for the cheaper cars produced by Daimler/BSA in 1912–14.

It is said that Armstrong-Siddeley had been left with a vast quantity of unwanted aeroengine cylinders on their hands as a result of a cancelled Government contract during the post-Armistice economy drive, and decided to build cheap cars to use them up. Whatever the source of its cylinders, the power unit of the Stoneleigh was a 90 degree aircooled vee-twin with bore and stroke measurements of 85×88mm, and a total capacity of just under a litre, with overhead valves and aluminium pistons. Claimed petrol consumption was 40 miles per gallon. Considering that the Stoneleigh was intended as a cheap car (its basic price in 1922 was £185, reduced by £30 the next year), it was unusual that it had an orthodox gearbox and spiral bevel final drive, as most vehicles in the sub-economy class got by with strengthened motor cycle transmissions.

Another surprising feature was that, although the original Stoneleighs had no self-starting equipment, by the end of 1923 the all-in price included a Bendix-drive electric starter, 'with automatic half-compression device'.

The usual coachwork was known as 'the open Utility body', in which the driver sat in splendid isolation in the centre of the car, with two passengers sitting abreast behind him.

For another £10 one could have the 'Chummy' body, with the steering moved from the centre of the car to the orthodox right-hand position and bucket seats set abreast for driver and passenger, with two occasional seats behind.

But in 1923 one could buy an Austin Seven, which looked much more like a real car, for the same price as a Chummy Stoneleigh, and by 1924 Armstrong Siddeley had given up the unequal struggle against the experienced mass-producers.

1924 GP Sunbeam

The Wolverhampton Sunbeam company had started racing in 1912 with a tuned version of their 3-litre production car: and won one of the top French races, the Coupe de l'Auto. Various racing models followed, including the first ever V-12 car, *Toddles V* of 1913, which had a modified 9-litre aeroengine.

After the 1914–18 war, Sunbeam continued racing, H. O. D. Segrave winning the 1923 French Grand Prix in a 2-litre six-cylinder car obviously copied from Fiat racing practice.

In 1924 a new model was produced – designed like the 1923 GP car by the Italian Bertiarone – which pioneered the modern practice of supercharging in which the supercharger draws in gas/air mixture through the carburetter and compresses it, rather than blowing through the carburetter intake. The twin-cam engine was both flexible and powerful, maximum output being quoted as being between 138 and 146bhp, and top speed as 125–130mph.

The first competition outing of this car was the French Grand Prix, held over a tricky three-mile course at Lyons. Sunbeam entered a team of three, driven by Segrave, Kenelm Lee Guinness and Dario Resta. They were up against formidable opposition: Delage had entered three V-12 cars, driven by René Thomas, Robert Benoist and Albert Divo; the immortal type 35 Bugatti was making its first appearance (five were entered); Alfa-Romeo's new cars were designed by Vittorio Jano on well-proved lines; Fiat's team of four was led by the veteran Felice Nazzaro, who had started racing nearly twenty years earlier; single entries were a cuff-valve Schmidt and a Miller driven by Count Lou Zborowski, the man responsible for building the Chitty-Chitty-Bang-Bangs.

In practice, the Sunbeams were noticeably faster than any of the other cars, and Segrave determined to go all out to win from the start. The night before the race, a representative of the Bosch Magneto company called on the Sunbeam team, and persuaded them to replace the old pattern Bosch magnetos on their cars with the later improved model: and the new magnetos were defective.

Segrave completed his first lap at an average speed of 70.15mph, keeping ahead of the rest of the field right through the next lap and most of the third. Then disaster struck, the car limped into the pits, misfiring badly, and dropped to seventeenth position while the sparking plugs were replaced. Throughout the race the Sunbeams were plagued by ignition trouble: Segrave also had to change mechanics, when a piece of tread from a burst tyre on another Sunbeam flew through the air and knocked out Marocchi, riding beside Segrave as was then the custom.

Segrave fought back desperately, clawing back through the pack between bouts of misfiring, and even setting up the fastest lap of the day (76.25mph) on the twenty-ninth lap. It was to no avail. He finished in fifth place, and the race went to Campari, driving one of the new Alfas.

1926 Bentley 3-litre

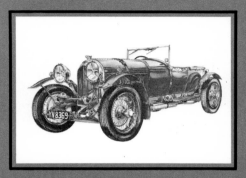

Although one naturally thinks of the 3-litre Bentley as the typical motorcar of the vintage years, it is instructive to note that while 132,000 cars were produced in 1925 in the United Kingdom, 54,151 of these were Bullnose Morrises and less than 400 were Bentleys. In fact the total output of Bentley Motors in their active life of a decade (1921–31) was only 3,061, less than the number of Morris cars produced on average during one *month* of 1925.

W. O. Bentley, who had already made a considerable name for himself with his fleet aluminium-pistoned DFPs of 1913–14 and his wartime Bentley Rotary aeroengines, had decided to produce a fast touring car of advanced, yet orthodox design, capable of covering great distances with complete reliability.

The power unit was a four-valve-per cylinder, single overhead camshaft engine with dimensions of 80×149mm, giving a swept volume of 2996cc, and developing some 80bhp at 3500rpm. The influence of the 1914 Grand Prix Mercedes on the design of the valve gear was apparent: Bentley did consider a twin–cam layout as pioneered by the 1912 Grand Prix Peugeot, and later used on the 1914 Tourist Trophy Humber (which was designed by his collaborator in developing the 3-litre, F. T. Burgess), but shelved it on account of the potential noise problems.

The prototype engine first ran in October 1919, and the complete car was on the road by December, but owing to the company's chronic lack of capital, production did not begin until the autumn of 1921.

From the start the company pursued – as finances permitted – an active racing policy, but it was with some reluctance that they allowed John Duff, a Bentley agent, to enter a 3-litre for a new 24-hour race that was being held at Le Mans in France: much to everyone's surprise it finished fourth, having made the fastest lap of the day, 66.69mph. From then on Le Mans became virtually a Bentley benefit: the marque won the *Vingt-quatre Heures du Mans* in 1924, 1927, 1928, 1929 and 1930.

Perhaps the most famous of the touring versions of the 3-litre was the Red Label (so-called because the winged 'B' on the radiator badge was on a red ground) with a 9ft 9.5in wheelbase, four-wheel brakes and a guaranteed speed in chassis form of 90mph. The engine, with twin bronze-bodied SU 'Sloper' carburetters, was based on the racing power units developed for the firm's entries in the 1922 Tourist Trophy Race: normal coachwork was a light four-seater tourer by Van den Plas of London.

It was a delightful car to drive, with firm, moderately heavy steering, excellent braking, a cone clutch with a particularly sweet action and a four-speed close-ratio gearbox that was a joy to use.

1927 Humber 14/40 Coupé

'As housewives can be house proud, so motorists can be car proud, and some of the proudest motorists I have met not only own Humbers, but the car before that was a Humber, and the one before that was also a Humber.

'The Humber firm must also have a motive in industry, and that is to retain the confidence of all their clients so that they can come again. It takes some doing with competition on a world plane, and there is something special in the job that inspires so great a loyalty.' Thus, in 1927, a motoring correspondent who cloaked his identity under the unimaginative pseudonym of 'Owner Driver' sought to explain the philosophy behind the Humber, by then become one of the more popular motorcars, with production running at around 4,000 cars a year justifying the firm's slogan 'Eminent among the best'.

Since the days of Thomas Humber, who had died in 1910, the Humber company had concentrated on the manufacture of honestly-built popular cars which gave excellent value for money, even if their price was a little higher than average.

Production had been concentrated on Coventry in 1908, when the Beeston works had closed for lack of capital; from an early date, all the new Coventry Humbers had four-speed gearboxes.

A new range, which threw off all vestiges of the old Coventry/ Beeston designs, appeared in 1913, and included one of the better cyclecars, the vee-twin Humberette, originally produced in air-cooled form only at £125, and later available with the option of watercooling at slight extra cost.

'Real' cars among the 1913 offerings were of 11, 14, 20 and 28hp —all four-cylinder models of conservative design, ranging in price from £285 to £490 in chassis form.

An out-of-character move was the building of a team of twin overhead camshaft racers on Peugeot lines for the 1914 Isle of Man Tourist Trophy. They were not particularly successful, and remain the only twin-cam machines ever to have borne the Humber name: their designer was F. T. Burgess, later to assist in producing the original 3-litre Bentley.

After the war the 10hp was continued, along with a 15.9hp model; the old sidevalve arrangement was replaced by an overhead inlet, side exhaust layout (which had a negligible effect on performance) in 1923, when, too, the charming little 8/18hp economy model made its introduction.

By 1926, the cars had become 9/20hp, 12/25hp and 15/40hp respectively: by 1927 a new model had replaced the 12/25, known as the 14/40, 'designed with a view to satisfying the needs of those who desire medium power and ample accommodation within moderate price limits (£460–£575)'. There was also a new 20/55hp six.

In 1928 Humber and Hillman were taken over to form the nucleus of the Rootes Group.

1927 Singer Senior 10/27

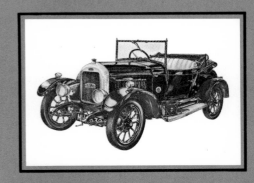

Like many enterprising young men of the mid-Victorian era George Singer (born in Sussex in 1847) sought his fortune in Coventry. He had worked with James ('Father of the Cycle Industry') Starley at the engineering firm of Penns, of Lewisham, Kent, and followed his colleague north, joining the sewing machine company he had founded.

Singer was a foreman at the Coventry Machinists Company in 1868 when Rowley B. Turner, nephew of the firm's manager, brought one of the new Michaux Velocipedes over from Paris, with orders for a further 400 similar machines to be built by his uncle's firm.

In 1875 George Singer left the company in order to set up his own business, in which he was partnered by his brother-in-law, J. E. Stringer. Singer improved the dubious steering characteristics of the old high-wheeled 'ordinary' bicycles by raking the forks so that a line drawn through the steering head struck the ground at the point of contact of the front wheel.

He also developed a treadle-driven 'Xtra Ordinary', on which the rider sat nearer the ground than usual—he built one 'Xtra Ordinary' with one treadle lever higher than the other so that his brother Robert, who had a short leg, could ride with ease.

Singer then constructed a 'Rational' bicycle, which had only a forty-nine-inch diameter front wheel—some makers had used 62inch or more—and a large rear wheel to add weight at the back and prevent nervous riders from taking a header over the handlebars.

George Singer was a man of some consequence in Coventry—he had been Mayor three times before ever the company turned to motor manufacture.

Their first venture was a motor cycle, the design of which they had acquired from Birch and Perks of Coventry. The power unit was contained inside the rear wheel, which it drove by gearing; the advantage of this self-contained 'Power Wheel' was that it could be applied indifferently to bicycles or tricycles, thus simplifying production. More substantial designs followed; in 1904 Singer built under licence a Lea-Francis-designed car (R. H. Lea was a former Singer employee) which had a three-cylinder overhead camshaft engine—in the interests of smooth running the connecting rods were thirty-nine inches long.

In 1912, following experiments with an air-cooled transverse-engined cyclecar, Singer introduced an excellent four-cylinder 1096cc car which sold well: a modernised version was made after the Great War and developed into the 'Senior' in 1926, as the even more diminutive 848cc 'Junior' had come on the scene. From 1928 many Singers had the ingenious 'Sunshine Saloon' coachwork, in which the roof of an apparently normal fabric saloon could be wound back in fine weather with a crankhandle. Invariably, when the rain began to fall, it would stick.

1928 Leyland-Thomas

'The only car we consider worth while as a sparring partner to the Leyland Eight is the Rolls-Royce.' Bold words, perhaps, but that was the considered opinion of John Godfrey Parry Thomas, the idiosyncratic Welshman whom Leyland Motors, hitherto producers of steam and petrol commercial vehicles, had given *carte blanche* to produce 'the most perfect car it is possible to design and manufacture' in 1917. His assistant was Reid Railton, who was later to design a number of famous successful land speed record and racing cars.

The Leyland Eight unveiled at the 1920 Olympia Motor Show, was the first complete motor car which Thomas had designed, although in 1907, aged 22, he had devised an ingenious electro-mechanical transmission, and during the war had developed a 350bhp aero engine with eight cylinders set in the shape of an 'X' (it seized-up on test due to hasty assembly).

The fact that the Leyland Eight was at one and the same time the most costly British motorcar and a completely original design which owed nothing to any car which had preceded it, was indicative of Thomas' genius.

The car which stole the show at Olympia in 1920 was the first British production straight eight-cylinder model (although the redoubtable Danny Weigel had fielded a team of straight-eights in the 1907 French Grand Prix with a singular lack of success). Like his contemporary, Ettore Bugatti, Parry Thomas had an eye for architectural detail, and the massive power unit of the Leyland Eight looked like masonry transmuted into metal. All the inlet and exhaust manifolding was carried inside the cylinder block, only a minimum of plumbing and piping disturbing the symmetry of the engine, which as designed had a bore and stroke of 89×140mm (6967cc), but was later increased to 89×146mm (7266cc). The single overhead camshaft was operated by triple eccentrics: like all Thomas' car designs (and his fame rests on only four models) the Eight has leaf valve springs serving each pair of inlet and exhaust valves. The engine which in standard form developed 120bhp at 2500rpm, and was developed (though not by Thomas) in its ultimate form to give 200bhp at 3800rpm, also featured a compressor for inflating the tyres.

The massive frame sidemembers were pierced for lightness (even so the bare chassis weighed 30cwt) and the rear suspension featured, for the first time ever, torsion bar assistance. In fact, the Leyland Eight positively bristled with originality wherever you looked, the result of which was that even at its chassis price of £1875 it was uneconomical to build.

About fourteen were built during Thomas' lifetime (he was killed attempting the Land Speed Record in 1927) and one, which still survives, was constructed from spare parts—and greatly modified in the process—in 1928–30.

1929 *Alvis*

The Alvis company had been building one-off front-wheel driven racing and hillclimb cars since 1925: their first effort, which made more use of duralumin than any previous car (and most succeeding ones)—even the chassis was pressed from this material, giving an all-up weight of 9.5cwt—was known as 'Tadpole' because its tail waggled so violently from side to side when in action. The lessons learned from these experimental cars gave Alvis the confidence to embark on the production of front-wheel-driven sports cars in 1928.

Low-slung and futuristically styled, the 12/75hp front-wheel-drive Alvis retailed at £550 in chassis form compared with £400 for the normal 12/50.

The 12/75 had a single overhead camshaft four-cylinder engine, with a swept volume of 1496cc (68 × 103mm): but the extra power promised by the overhead camshaft didn't materialise, for in un-blown form the unit had exactly the same output as the standard 12/50, for a lot of extra complication. So a supercharger was available as an optional fitting, which boosted the power to 75bhp. It also gave the engine a dipsomaniac thirst: if one peered down the cavernous choke of the big bronze Solex carburetter when the engine was on full song, one could see a fountain of neat petrol gushing out of the jet and vanishing into the maw of the engine.

The motoring press was seduced by the technical features of the new Alvis: its all-round independent suspension, its supercharger, its roadholding and its advanced styling.

What they did not stress was the fact that this was virtually a road-going racing car, and that it required a new driving technique which was quite foreign to the average motorist of the 1920s. They also omitted to point out that the engine was awkward to work on, could be difficult to start, and that its timing gears were far noisier than one would expect on a touring car, and were virtually unbearable to the ear when a saloon body was fitted.

Orders poured in. Alvis profits soared to a record £46,134 for 1928, and the front-wheel-drive cars found their way into the hands of owners to whose requirements they were obviously quite un-suited—one was even sold to a clergyman who used it for visiting his parishioners. Other faults were revealed, such as a regrettable tendency for two gears to engage at once, causing a disastrous derangement of the gearbox's internal economy.

The sales figures persuaded Alvis to drop the well-tried 12/50 temporarily but the shortcomings of the 12/75 front-wheel-drive car in the hands of ordinary motorists, rather than the enthusiasts for whom it was really intended, caused the company to revert quickly to the production of conventional cars.

1931/32 Bugatti Type 51

Ettore Bugatti was an artist as well as an engineer: indeed, had not his brother Rembrandt been a well-known sculptor, Bugatti would almost certainly have followed that calling rather than that of motor manufacture. As it was, Ettore Bugatti produced cars which for sheer elegance of line have never been equalled. His earlier designs all bore the mark of Bugatti's original approach to motor building. The cars were constructed in a factory of almost clinical cleanliness on Bugatti's feudally run estate at Molsheim, Alsace; the works were small, but equipped with the latest in machine tools.

In 1924 there appeared what has often been referred to as his crowning achievement: the 2-litre straight-eight Type 35 Grand Prix model. The engine was a square-sided aluminium monobloc, of relatively complex construction, and relied on the tremendous standards of workmanship employed in the Bugatti factory to make it work. While the engine had a complex ball and roller bearing crankshaft, it employed a crude lubrication system in which oil was squirted through jets on to the crank and splashed everywhere: restricted or even non-existent water jacketing round the hottest parts of the engine made cooling a somewhat empirical process. Moreover, the firing order was unique, being 1-5-2-6-3-7-4-8, for Bugatti does not seem to have grasped the need for smooth power output from an eight-cylinder engine: but his ignition sequence probably contributed much to the unique exhaust note of the Bugatti, a vivid tearing crackle which cannot adequately be described in words. The chassis, too, was unique. In elevation, its cross-section varied continuously from dumb-irons to tail, from a delicate 0.75in at the front to 6.75in at the centre of the frame. In plan, too, the chassis varied in width, following the contours of the elegant pointed-tail racing body, inside which the forward pointing rear quarter-elliptic springs (inspired, it is rumoured, by the suspension of a Cockney coster barrow) were entirely concealed.

The flat-spoked aluminium wheels incorporating the brake drums were another Bugatti first: drawing them off laid bare the brake shoes, rendering adjustment or replacement as easy as possible under racing conditions.

Unorthodox, the Type 35 may have been, but it was an undoubted success, almost despite Bugatti's idiosyncratic design features. Top speed was over 120mph in its later, 2.3-litre Type 35B form: a 1.5-litre version was also made. During the late 1920s, when international racing was in the doldrums following unwisely frequent changes of formula, Type 35s won perhaps 2000 major and minor races: the final development of the design was the Type 51 of 1931, which retained the basic layout, but featured a new 2.3-litre twin overhead camshaft engine, and could be tuned to exceed 130mph; this engine was subsequently fitted to the Type 55 roadster.

1933 1·5-litre Aston Martin

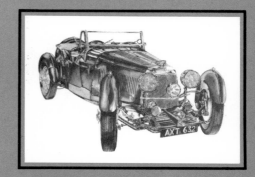

In 1911, Paul Braham, proprietor of a small motor repair works in Henniker Mews, Kensington, sold his business to Hesse & Savory, general engineers of Teddington, and joined a company that was just beginning to produce a 12hp car called the Palladium, the most distinctive feature of which was its slogan: 'The salvation of Troy was the possession of the Palladium (see legend); the salvation of motorists from all trouble is the possession of a Palladium.'

Hesse & Savory apparently failed to make a go of their new acquisition, and in 1912 disposed of it to one of their directors, Robert Bamford, and an old cycling colleague of his, Lionel Martin. Martin, much impressed by the new Bugatti light car, decided to build an English equivalent, initially for his own amusement and as a foil to his 40/50hp Rolls-Royce.

His initial experiments consisted of coaxing as much performance as possible out of a 10hp Singer, and this gave him much data on camshaft profiles: he was especially successful at Brooklands and at Aston Clinton hill-climb.

Then, in 1913, he acquired the chassis of a 1908 Isotta-Fraschini, a 1.4-litre light car designed by Guistino Cattaneo, a brilliant Italian of the same stamp as Bugatti: in this frame his mechanic, Frank Hunt, installed a Coventry-Simplex engine of 10hp, with lightweight steel Zephyr pistons. Before any real development could be carried out on this car, the war broke out.

After the Armistice, Martin began limited production of cars, under the name Aston Martin to celebrate the hill-climbing successes of his 1912 Singer. The prototype, with a 1486cc sidevalve engine, was completed in late 1919, and was the first car to climb the notorious 1:2.5 gradient of Alms Hill, near Henley-on-Thames.

In 1922, backed by the legendary Count Louis Zborowski, the company constructed a number of twin overhead camshaft racing cars with engines like 1.5-litre versions of the prewar Grand Prix Peugeots: they were not entirely successful, but the achievements of the racing Astons were sufficient to establish the reputation of the company, which was always plagued by insufficient finances. Then, in 1924, Zborowski was killed racing at Monza, and the capital dried up altogether. After building perhaps sixty cars, Aston Martin failed.

In 1926 the name was acquired by A. C. Bertelli, who designed an all-new car, still of 1.5-litres, with coachwork by his brother: possibly twenty cars of this type were built between 1926 and 1929 when a new factory at Feltham was acquired. These 'International Sports' Astons had, oddly enough, worm final drive, and were rather heavily built: but in their most highly developed forms, the Le Mans and the Mark II Ulster, they were very fine cars indeed.

1934 Singer 9 Le Mans

In 1932 Singer introduced a sporting version of their popular 9hp model, which had a 972cc engine with a bore and stroke of 60 × 86mm and an overhead camshaft. That year one of these cars won a Coupe des Glaciers in the arduous Alpine Trial, and another was entered in the 1933 Le Mans 24-hour race where it qualified for an award after a steady run at an average of 50 mph.

Thereafter a variety of sporting Singers was produced by the company but the true Le Mans Model had a very special engine, capable of 6000rpm, with a counterbalanced crankshaft, ribbed aluminium sump and high-lift cams. Other features of the specification included twin horns, twin spare wheels, twin dash lamps and twin windscreen wipers. Price of the two-seater Le Mans was £215 in 1933, compared with £185 for the standard four-seater sports.

By 1935 the cost of the Le Mans had risen to £425, while the ordinary speed two-seater cost £215: but that same year a team of three cars was entered for the Irish Tourist Trophy, run on the Ards circuit.

As was fairly common practise at that time, the cars had springs in the drag links to cushion road shock at the ball-joints. To make the steering more precise, the drivers—among whom was the Sports Editor of *The Autocar*, S. C. H. Davis, a former Bentley works driver—removed these springs, making the joint solid.

The cars went well, keeping up with the rest of the field, and even gaining a little on one fast corner. Then Singer No. 38 ran amok on that bend, rammed the bank, and was out of the race. Soon after, Sammy Davis entered the bend, only to find the car suddenly fail to respond to the steering wheel. His Singer swerved across the track, savaged the bank, rose up on its tail and turned over, hitting its team-mate in the process. Davis escaped with only a scratch on his head, incurred when his helmet was knocked off on the bodywork of the other car.

Finally, the third car in the team crashed at exactly the same spot: it transpired that removing the cushioning spring from the drag link had placed an intolerable strain on the ball-joint, which fractured. That this should have happened on the same bend to all three cars was an unfortunate coincidence that did the reputation of the Le Mans no good at all: nor did it enhance the image of its big brother, the six-cylinder 1.5-litre model, introduced in 1933. The Le Mans was listed until 1937, in which year a works car took fourth place in the Tourist Trophy. Although Singer subsequently listed 'Roadster' models of apparent sporting mien, these were rather depressing machines, and vastly inferior to the MGs they were intended to rival.

1898 Star-Benz

D

1898 Star-Benz

Single cylinder 110mm by 110mm; 1050cc;
two-speed belt primary drive, chain final
drive; 3.5 RAC horsepower.

1901 Godiva 9hp dos-à-dos

1901 *Godiva 9hp dos-à-dos*

Built by Paynes & Bates, Coventry,
Warwickshire. Two-cylinder front-mounted
9hp engine. Similar cars were sold to
R. M. Wright of Lincoln, who marketed
them under the name Stonebow.

©1970 National Magazine Co. Ltd. Drawn
exclusively for CAR by Peter Griffin from
the original in the Herbert Art Gallery &
Museum, Coventry.

1903 De Dion Bouton

1903 De Dion Bouton

One cylinder, bore 90mm; stroke 110mm;
6hp, two forward gears, no reverse.

1904 8hp Rover

1904 8hp Rover

One cylinder, 114mm by 130mm; tubular aluminium backbone chassis; metal to metal clutch; three-speed gearbox with reverse.

1905 Humber

1905 Humber

Four cylinders in line, water cooled, 80mm bore, 96mm stroke, 2050cc; coil ignition, 8/10hp RAC; three-speed gearbox with reverse; live rear axle.

©1969 National Magazine Co. Ltd. Drawn exclusively for CAR by Peter Griffin from the original in the Herbert Art Gallery and Museum, Coventry.

1907 TT Model Rover

1907 TT Model Rover

Four cylinders, 97mm by 110mm, 3252cc; three forward gears; transverse front suspension, semi-elliptic rear.

1907 Rover

1907 Rover

One cylinder, 114mm by 130mm; 8hp
RAC; three forward gears and reverse; side
lever gear change; metal to metal clutch;
fuel range 160 miles.

1908 Riley Tourer 12/18

1908 Riley Tourer 12/18

V-twin engine, 102mm by 127mm; 2075cc, 12.9hp; three-speed gearbox and reverse; HT magneto; semi-elliptic springs front and rear.

©1967 National Magazine Co. Ltd. Drawn exclusively for CAR by Peter Griffin from the original in the Herbert Art Gallery and Museum, Coventry.

1909 Maudslay 17hp

1909 Maudslay 17hp

Four cylinders, 90mm by 130mm; leather faced cone clutch running in oil bath; foot brake on propeller shaft, hand brake on rear drums; thermo syphon cooling; worm drive live axle, four-speed gearbox and reverse; semi-elliptic front springs, three-quarter elliptic rear springs.

1910 7hp Swift

1910 7hp Swift

One cylinder, bore 105mm, stroke 127mm, side valves; HT magneto ignition with battery and trembler coil for starting; cast iron bearings for crankshaft and gearbox shafts; cone clutch, three speeds. Bevel gear final drive.

1911 Daimler

1911 Daimler

Six cylinders, sleeve valves, 3921cc, 23hp; bore 80mm, stroke 130mm; three forward gears; brakes foot on rear, hand on transmission.

1911 Austin Town Carriage

1911 Austin Town Carriage

Four cylinders, 88mm by 114mm, 19.6hp
RAC; four-speed gearbox with reverse;
1911 purchase price £475.

©1968 National Magazine Co. Ltd. Drawn
exclusively for CAR by Peter Griffin from
the original at the BMC showroom, Solihull.

1912 Rover Landaulet

1912 Rover Landaulet

Four cylinders, 75mm by 130mm, 2298cc, 12hp; three-speed gearbox and reverse; HT magneto; semi-elliptic springs front and rear.

1912 Benz Grand Tourer

1912 Benz Grand Tourer

Four cylinders, 185mm by 200mm, 21.5 litres; 200bhp at 1600rpm; cone clutch, separate gearbox and bevel drive; chain final drive; transmission footbrake, rear drum handbrake; maximum speed 120mph.

1912 Crouch Carette 8hp

1912 Crouch Carette 8hp

V-twin, water cooled, 85mm by 90mm,
1018cc; Thermoid-lined cone clutch, three-
speed gearbox, chain drive to rear wheel.

©1969 National Magazine Co. Ltd. Drawn
exclusively for CAR by Peter Griffin from
the original in the Herbert Art Gallery and
Museum, Coventry.

1912 Turner 10hp

1912 Turner 10hp

Four cylinders, bore 69mm, stroke 110mm;
three-speed box and reverse; three-place
bench seat; footbrake on rear drums, hand
on transmission.

©1970 National Magazine Co. Ltd. Drawn
exclusively for CAR by Peter Griffin from
the car owned by Turner Manufacturing Co.
of Wolverhampton.

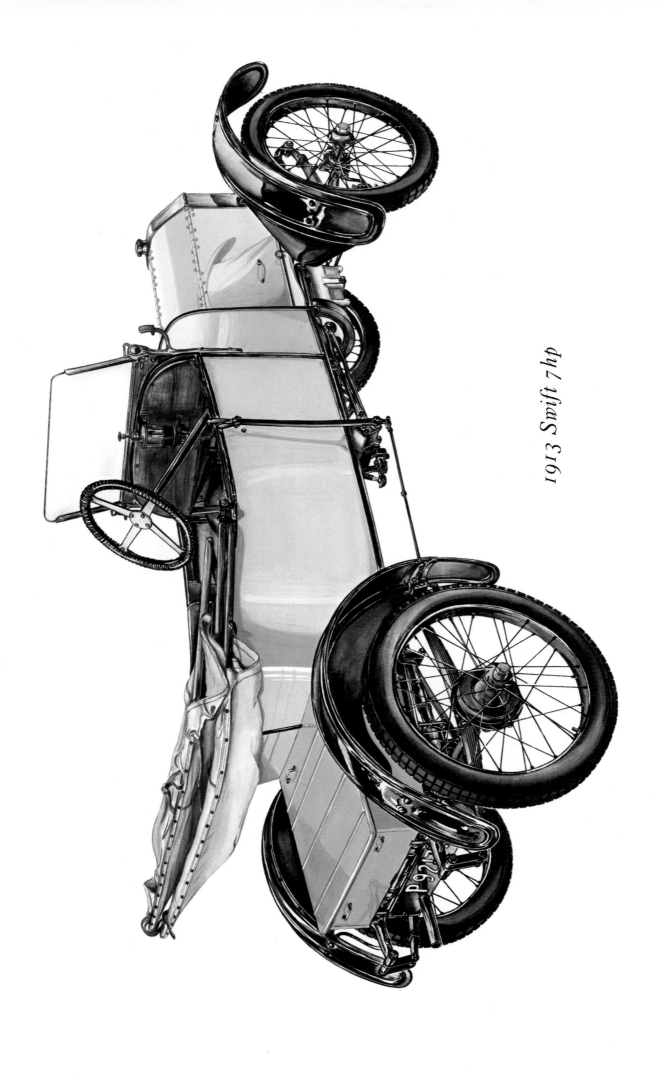

1913 Swift 7 hp

1913 Swift 7hp

Two cylinders, 80mm by 130mm; side valves; HT magneto ignition; cone clutch, three-speed gearbox and reverse, bevel geared live axle.

©1970 National Magazine Co. Ltd. Drawn exclusively for CAR by Peter Griffin from the original at the Herbert Art Gallery and Museum, Coventry.

1913 Arden

1913 Arden

Two cylinders, 85mm by 95mm, 1092cc; three-speed gearbox; leather-lined cone clutch; shaft and bevel gear final drive.

©1969 National Magazine Co. Ltd. Drawn exclusively for CAR by Peter Griffin from the original in the Herbert Art Gellery and Museum, Coventry (Owned by M. R. J. Edwards).

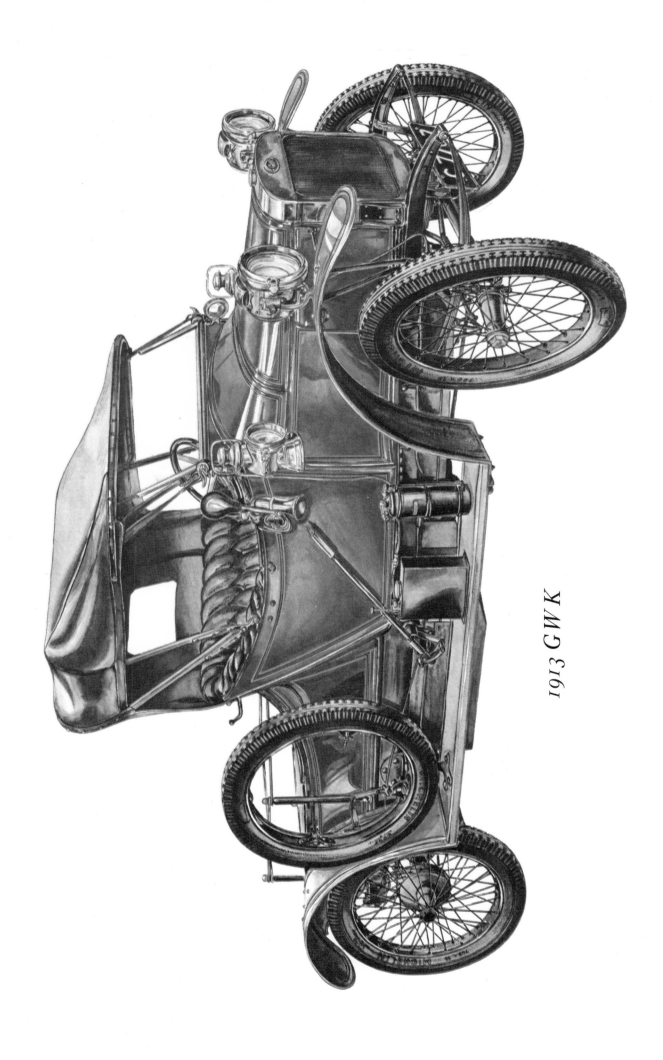

1913 GWK

1913 GWK

Two cylinders, 86mm by 92mm; 1069cc; infinitely variable friction disc transmission arranged for four forward gears and reverse; HT magneto; 55mph, 45mpg.

1913 Morris - Oxford

1913 Morris-Oxford

Four cylinders, 60mm by 90mm, 1018cc; 10hp; three-speed gearbox with reverse; Bosch ZF 4 magneto; side valve; 16.4bhp at 2400rpm.

©1968 National Magazine Co. Ltd. Drawn exclusively for CAR by Peter Griffin from the original in the Herbert Gallery and Museum, Coventry.

1921 Rover 8hp

1921 Rover 8hp

Two cylinders, air cooled, 85mm by 88mm,
capacity 998cc; single disc fabric clutch,
three-speed gearbox; open Cardan shaft
to worm drive rear axle; drum brakes
on rear wheels.

©1968 National Magazine Co. Ltd. Drawn
exclusively for CAR by Peter Griffin from
the original at the Rover Co. Ltd. Museum,
Solihull.

1921 10/30 Alvis

1921 10/30 Alvis

Four cylinders, 65mm by 110mm, 1455cc; four-speed gearbox with reverse; Solex Special carburetter, maximum speed over 60mph.

©1968 National Magazine Co. Ltd. Drawn exclusively for CAR by Peter Griffin from the original in the possession of the Alvis Car Co. Coventry.

1924 Stoneleigh 9hp

1924 Stoneleigh 9hp

Two cylinders, 90deg vee, air cooled, 85mm bore by 88mm stroke, 999cc; three-speed gearbox, spiral bevel rear axle.

1924 GP Sunbeam

1924 GP Sunbeam

Six cylinders in two blocks of three, 67mm by 94mm, 1988cc, supercharged, 146bhp at 5000rpm; four forward gears, multiplate clutch, bevel rear axle; four wheel drum brakes with mechanical servo; top speed 125mph.

1926 Bentley 3-litre

1926 Bentley 3-litre

Four cylinders, single ohc, 80mm by 180mm, 85bhp; four-speed gearbox, reverse; servo-assisted brakes; Van den Plas four-seat open bodywork.

1927 Humber 14/40 Coupé

1927 Humber 14/40 Coupé

Four cylinders, 2050cc, 40bhp at 3000rpm; side exhaust valves, overhead inlet valves; four-speed gearbox, cone clutch; four-wheel brakes.

©1970 National Magazine Co. Ltd. Drawn exclusively for CAR by Peter Griffin from the car owned by W. J. Marshall at the Herbert Art Gallery and Museum.

1927 Singer Senior 10/27

1927 Singer Senior 10/27

Four cylinders, 69mm bore, 51.05mm stroke; 11.9hp, capacity 1571cc; Rotax variable magneto; three-speed gearbox and reverse; Solex horizontal carburetter.

© 1970 National Magazine Co. Ltd. Drawn exclusively for CAR by Peter Griffin from the original owned by H. E. N., Farnborough and kept at the Herbert Art Gallery and Museum, Coventry.

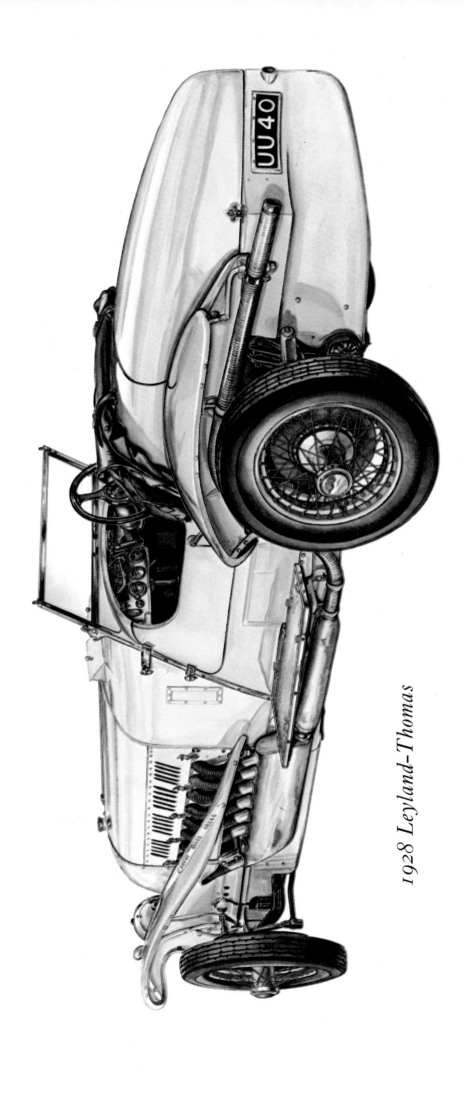

1928 Leyland-Thomas

1928 Leyland-Thomas

Eight cylinders, 89mm by 140mm, 6290cc; 200bhp at 2800rpm; four-speed gearbox; four-wheel brakes; semi-elliptic springs at front, located by radius rods quarter-elliptic (originally torsion-bar assisted) springs at rear.

1929 Alvis

1929 Alvis

Four cylinders, 68mm by 102mm, 1482cc; 75bhp supercharged, 50bhp unsupercharged; four forward gears and reverse; front wheel drive.

©1968 National Magazine Co. Ltd. Drawn exclusively for CAR by Peter Griffin from the original in the possession of the Alvis Motor Company.

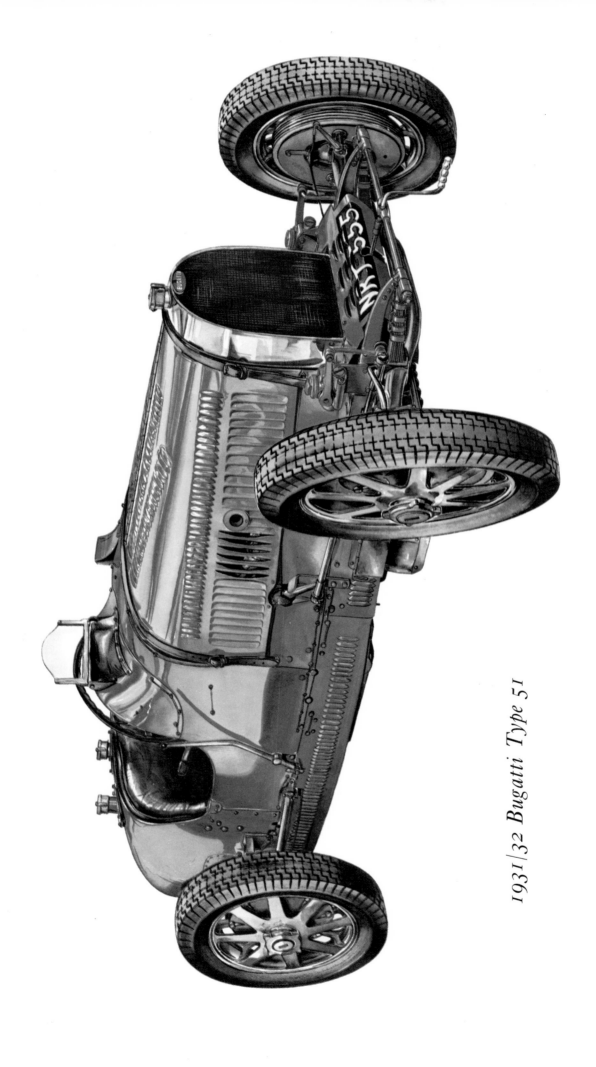

1931/32 Bugatti Type 51

1931/32 Bugatti Type 51

Eight cylinders, 60mm by 100mm, 2270cc supercharged, 18hp RAC; twin ohc; four-speed gear box.

1933 1·5-litre Aston Martin

1933 1.5-litre Aston Martin

Four cylinders, bore 69mm, stroke 99mm, overhead camshaft, two SU carburetters, four-speed gearbox and reverse.

©1970 National Magazine Co. Ltd. Drawn exclusively for CAR by Peter Griffin at the Birmingham Museum of Science and Industry from the car owned by D. M. Taylor.

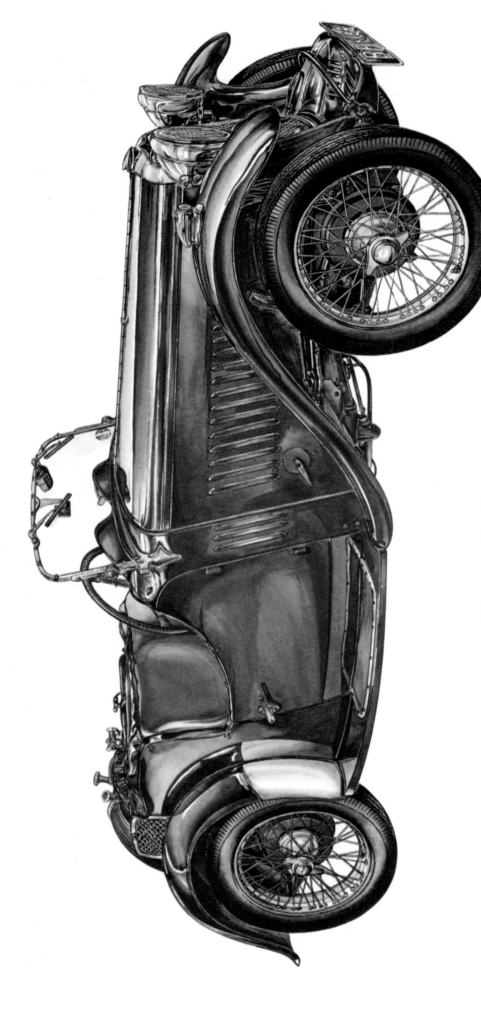

1934 Singer 9 Le Mans

8